PTSD is a 4 Letter Word

E. M. McConnell

This is a dark poetry collection and as such may have themes that are not suitable to all readers. For details of possible content and trigger warnings please refer to the Introduction

This collection is dedicated to all those who have wondered if they too have pieces missing. You don't. You're great just as you are.

Other Poetry Collections

Introduction

All the raw, ugly and angry stuff is right here. If my future self had told me I would be publishing this, I would have laughed at them.

I have written most of these over the last five or more years but have always felt they were too raw, too ugly, or too angry to be put in a poetry volume.

But poetry is not always meant to be beautiful, abstract and comforting. Sometimes it needs to be jagged and hard. Sometimes it needs to mean something. There are a lot of ugly subjects in this volume, and it will not suit everyone. I write about my past, and it is not pretty. Because of my past I live with C-PTSD, a brain disorder, dissociation, and sometimes depression. When I was young I also lived with disordered eating, self-harming and self-medicating with alcohol.

These are my scars written on pages. Is it pretty? No. But it is true. And perhaps it might bring you something too, to read this. I survived it. You probably survived it too. Or you will survive it, if you are living it now.

This is a dark collection of poetry. There are the following content warnings:
Assault
Sexual Assault
Mental Health
Sexual harassment
Domestic violence
Emotional Abuse
Intrusive thoughts
Self harm
Eating Disorders

Contents

My Head
is a
Battlefield

One Woman

I am one woman
  Just one body
  A flawed one
  Carrying a brain
  And a soul
  And some pain
  But really I am
  Legion
  In the selves
  That I have been
  Like reflections
  Overlapping in time

  The child who
  Had no parents
  To speak of
  Who was shunted
  From foster care

To grandparents
And back again
Who built her world
Inside her own head
To live in
When times were hard

The child with no memories
Who dreamed her way
Through school
So she did not have to see
The sympathetic faces
Of her teachers
Because they knew
She never told them
But they knew anyway

The teen who
Was homeless
And hurting herself
With knives and booze
Who didn't know better
Than to let people
Do what they wanted
With her body
Because they did
What they wanted
Whether you said yes or no

They did it anyway

The woman who
Tried to put things in order
To be the perfect
Student and Academic
The perfect girlfriend
Who hid her trauma
In a wine glass
Behind glassy eyes
And a wide lipsticked smile
Because it was easier
And people don't like
To hear about that anyway

The mother who
Learned about brain science
And Attachment Theory
So she could learn
How to actually parent
This helpless creature
That somehow she had grown
Wanting something to love her

But not understanding that
Parenting is about giving
All the love away
Even if you're empty

Not about getting something back
And she feared being
Just another abuser
But the child needed loving
So she loved it anyway

The woman who
Never looks in the mirror
And ignores the scars
Trying to stitch together
Memories that aren't there
From the past
And weaves them into
Pages of rage
So she can feel peace
And believe sometimes
That it doesn't matter anyway

The woman who
Always has fancy words to write
But has none
When she needs them
For the hard questions
And when people need to see
That she can feel
So she hides away
As she doesn't matter anyway

One woman
A thousand doubts
A soul of trauma
A mountain of mourning
A legion of selves

But this woman
Stands tall
And says that
It does matter
That this woman
Does matter anyway.

Cracked Porcelain

Smooth skin
   That you can run
   Your fingertips over
   A glacial journey
   Cold to the touch
   Perfect. Flawless
   Do not stray from
   The known track
   Only touch what I
   Allow you to see
   Never deviate
   Do not look at
   The cracks
   At my scars

Untitled

Fragmented fog flies
   Taking pieces of memory
   Floating by so slowly
   I open my hands wide
   Uncurling fingers
   And I watch them fly away
   Taking flight.

Eating.
Disordered.

Rules march before my eyes
  Useless slogans chirp
  Blinking merrily
  It doesn't help the fear
  The obsession
  Food, Calories. Fear.

  Hunger is a wild animal
  It roars between my ears
  Dizziness subsiding
  Weariness rising
  I feel my skin retract
  My cheekbones
  Hollowing in need

  I admire it when
  Nobody is looking
  I inspect my lists

Secretly drawn up
From whispered
Conversations

Overheard chatter
How to lose more weight
Be thin be thin be thin
And I cradle my hunger
As if it were a newborn
Sshh, I croon. I rock.

Can Cold Make A Statue?

The cold moisture seeping on glass
  Leaves a sheen of mystery there
  A delicate frosting to shield
  The jewelled, jaded ruby depths
  What can I find there?
  Certainly not the answers I seek
  Nor the understanding that I lack
  Nor the laughter that was stolen away

  But the chill touches my fingertips
  And my eager, waiting lips
  Snaking down past my throat
  And cooling my bones within

  I crave the chill, I crave the cold
  To be frozen solid from without
  For my hair to still and solidify
  For my eyes to glaze over in stone

For my hands to rest and still.

I surrender myself to it in hope
Welcoming the spreading blight
Calling out to Cold's sister, Oblivion
To reach out her arms again.

White Threads Float

White silk floats in the cool breeze
Coiling in arcs, folding over my mouth
Binding my words away, into oblivion
Cold water plunges into my brain
Freezing the neurons still in shock
My thoughts stutter and stop.

Threads flutter helpless in the air
Flayed by the sharp silver blade
That I hold in my still shaking hand
I float away from my festering roots
My mouth still bound by soothing silk
My brain hibernating in water cold
And the threads of my past dream away.

Hollow

Hollow eyes gaping out
  From hard sockets, empty and cold
  Trailing avenues of grief seared
  In a downward spiral from my eyes
  Those eyes that dried themselves out
  And then left in a self-imposed exile
  A hollow mouth ripped out at the seams
  Sinews and tissue crumbling
  As they mourn the dying of my smile
  My laugh falling
  Into bitter silence
  Hollow hands that turn
  Covering a desiccated rotting mouth
  That has nothing left to say
  And eyes that are now shadows
  That cried their pain away.

Envy

I look at the women
   And I feel my envy rise
   I count the visible bones
   I crave their look
   Hungrily

   If I had visible hip bones like that
   My life would be better
   I look at the women
   And I wish for it
   What they have
   Perfect bodies
   No awful skin and fat
   Getting in the way
   Making you feel slow
   Heavy

   I look at the women

And I see their normal
Beautiful bodies
Just being bodies with a soul
And I am happy for them
I wish I could be like that

I harbour a dark secret
I crave more than a diet
Or a weight loss
I know that even 40 pounds
Or more
Would not be enough

I want nothing. I want merely
My bones with skin stretched
On a frame
Or less
I want to be formless

A soul who can fly free
Without a body
Holding me down
Nothing to tether me here
Nothing that people can touch
Or take captive
Just a soul in the sky.

A Worm In My Brain

I call it a worm
  And perhaps it will be offended
  But I do not have a name for it
  Really
  It just is

  We haven't been introduced formally
  And we don't really have conversations
  More, it yells sometimes in my head
  With an overlay of loud music
  And my brain fries, stuttering
  Under the commands that make such sense
  You could hang yourself from that, there
  It whispers to me

  Nobody would know, not for hours
  And it's right. They wouldn't.
  I do not, though. The worm

Has no control over me.
Or at least I hope not.

Sometimes it screams into existence
When I speak too much, exposing something
And the noise drives up to a volume
Where I cannot think
And my brain staggers into silence
I weave drunkenly
Looking for guidance

Which only comes from it
The Worm
So I shut down, in panic
Removing myself from everything
And then I turn for guidance
But I meet empty silence
And cold air where the Worm was

I do not know what to do
I do not know if it is a friend or a foe
It feels not like a psychosis
Not a delusion as I see naught
But I hear. Maybe I am mad
I tell myself.

Just not in the glamorous way.
I listen, helplessly, to the silence

As the shrieking car-crash of my life
Has paused for a moment
And my unwanted visitor has gone.
I feel... lonely.

Untethering

I drop out of things
  Carefully, one by one
  Unpeeling myself
  So they leave no trace
  On my skin.

  I'm sorry, I email
  I need to drop out
  I don't think I can do this
  It was a mistake
  And I watch the idea
  Slowly float away

  But I know deep down
  That I am untethering
  The wrong things
  In order to avoid
  The elephant in the room

Do I need to
Untether myself
From love
Or do I need to
Just untether myself?

Untitled

I stare at a blank screen
   Headphones in my ears
   To muffle the sounds
   I can't bear to listen
   To music

   My mind is empty
   My eyes are full
   And burning
   My hands shake
   My throat yearns
   To take back the words

   My mouth locks shut
   Life is hard sometimes
   I need to lock myself
   Away from it
   I need to burn my hopes

And rip them out
At the roots.

Wearing The Wax

The wax melted to make
  A frozen face set smooth
  A perfect imitative mask
  Something to hide behind.

  The mask looks out calmly
  And my feelings slide inside
  But they are unseen.
  The anger can ripple out
  Under the wax but the mask
  Is undeterred. It stays.

  Tears don't melt it
  No matter how hot they fall
  Only a laugh might
  Rip the mask at the seams
  As my mouth stretches wide
  In unexpected mirth

But today the mask is strong
Set against my skin so closely
And my emotions slide behind
For nobody to see.

That's Me

I am a missing fragment
   That I have mislaid
   Like a web search
   That is incomplete
   And so it whirs away
   Gently to itself
   Never completing
   That's me

   Pieces stitched together
   With no memories between
   Emotions stuffed into pockets
   That I do not understand
   And my heart is smothered
   By angry voices
   Who tell me what I am
   That's me

I'm Waiting For It

When tears roll so free
  Down my cheeks yet
  I do not know
  If I cry for my broken past
  Or my nonexistent future

  I feel my life running out
  As if the sands are low
  I can hear it ticking slow
  It is not from fear
  Or from events that break me

  It's just a growing certainty
  That soon I need to say
  Alright this is it
  And end everything
  With just a sorry.

I don't even want to
It terrifies me to think
Of how I must do it

But yet the certainty remains
It is not what I want
But it is what must be
And who can argue with that?

Crying

When tears roll so free
  Down my cheeks yet
  I do not know
  If I cry for my broken past
  Or my non-existent future

If

If life is so perfect
   And full of promise
   Why does it always
   Feel like it is the end?

Still

I am a spider I think
  Drawing people in
  Breaking them
  Good people going bad
  I create the red flags
  Good people become
  Dangerous
  I am not good around
  Good people

  I must
  Hibernate
  Stay away
  My taint
  Don't corrupt them
  They all agree
  My poison taints
  I'm not a good person

Maul Me

Sharp teeth slavering hot
  Breath biting, tearing deep
  The pain consumes me
  In lightning white intensity
  But within my agony
  That I beg to be freed from
  There rises a stark focus
  A returning to life and reality
  Pain lets me breathe again
  It reminds me how to feel
  And sometimes that is a relief
  To break free of my cage
  Of white anaesthesia
  The numbing blind dark
  So it's pain, I'll take it
  If it helps me feel something
  Maul me, I whisper. More.

Hypervigilance: A Super Power

I sit with my back to a wall
  I might be sitting and laughing
  Casually swirling a wine glass
  But if you asked me right now
  I could tell you what everyone
  In the entire room is doing
  And how much of a threat they are.

  I never get drunk
  I might appear it
  But at an instant I sober up
  Ready
  Just in case
  Especially if I get to
  Work off some karmic debt
  And help someone else.
  Save them.

My shadow self rides behind my eyes
Ready to step out
If someone gets too close
Giving me an excuse to get feral
To unleash the dark
Loosening the leash
On the blood-lust
And my jaws snap shut
In anticipation of the kill.

You're always waiting for it
You say
It might not happen!
You say
Oh you young fool.
It already did.
You need to relax!
You say
I laugh.

Hypervigilance
Is a super power
I say.
It's a shame you
Don't have it.
The wall feels strong
Against my back
As I swirl my glass.

Hallucination

Work beckons
  I'm thinking of the train
  Pulling into the station
  The first of two to catch
  I'm thinking of
  My classes and what I need
  It wars with my lack of sleep
  The street is normal
  Until it is not

  Fragmenting into a
  World of unreality
  The car next to me
  Shivering and rising up
  On its haunches
  Headlights blazing
  Bumpers curling
  In an approximation

Of a roar

I feel the sharp branches
Of the hedges in my back
My breath hitching
Heart racing
My fear rising
And the car curls its smile
Grinning, sardonically.
The train. I have to get the train
Not loiter in a bush

I run, not looking back
Not stopping
Just don't think about it
If you don't tell
It didn't happen.

Brain Bites

Brain lurching forward
  With no off switch
  Reeling through a myriad
  Of nightmare scenarios
  Technicolour dreams
  Demanding that I face them
  Eyes taped open
  Accept the scenario
  Live it
  How will you feel?

  Eyes wide
  Face flinching
  Unable to look away
  Death plays the film reel
  Small dead bodies
  Buried under a white sheet
  My brain fractures

Shattering under the strain
My heart sickening
Mouth moving silently
But this has not happened yet

Trauma floods my brain
It dances in it maniacally
And my body bears the brunt
The pain of fear festering
In my limbs
My fingers hurting
My cheekbones burning

The sane part of my brain
Picks itself up with reason
This is not real
It is hypothetical
My heart still races
The hysteria screams
I still my gasps
Do not borrow trouble
I remind myself
Lest it arrives.

When It Isn't

It's not real.
  Just wishing it does not
  Make it so.
  It never will be real
  None of us get a happy ending
  It is not that we do not deserve it
  We fought the lions
  Overcoming the odds
  But still there is no movie ending
  There will never be
  Someone who sees us for who we are
  Nobody to run up
  And say I see you

  Forgotten goods will always
  Lie still in the night
  Helpless
  Not saved at

The Eleventh Hour
But quietly left
It is time to stop
Hoping.

Face

I don't look in the mirror
   My face turns away from it
   Contorts to avoid it in fact
   Mirrors are my nemesis

   I do not like to look
   The expressions and features
   That belonged to my abusers
   I hate seeing it on my own face
   A face that moves like they do
   That reflects what they say
   Their expressions.
   Their hate

   Why would I want to like this face?
   A skinsuit foisted onto me
   A constant reminder
   Of jeers and lust thrown

By strangers
Of beatings and glares
By those who loved me
I look away. I care not to see it
That face that reflects my past.

I

I'm the problem
   It is me
   My darkness
   Poison seeping
   I make good people bad
   Watching soulful eyes turn

   Smiles turn to
   Aggression
   My soul is venom
   I need to change
   Be better
   Do better
   There has to be
   A way to solve the problem
   Being me

Drowning

Where were they
  People like me who
  Could save me from myself
  Once
  Can someone
  Save me from myself
  I am destroying myself
  I am destroying myself
  Peeling my skin
  In a hysteric phase
  Trying to get at the good soul
  Within
  The myth
  It's always a myth

Common Denominator

White wall
  Tear burning hot
  Hands clasped
  Throat closing
  It happens
  Just as
  It always
  Did before
  Common
  Denominator
  Is not you
  It could never be you
  But it is me
  The common
  Denominator
  Is me

My Scars

The Psych Ward

There were so many doors
  Clanging shut behind me
  Locks and keys
  And blank faces
  Of turnkeys in bright shirts
  Who ushered me in
  And locked the door behind me.

  I wasn't there for me
  I was there for you
  Having taken you for help
  They signed the papers
  To take your freedom away
  To fill you with drugs
  That will help you they said

  The Doctor eyed me meaningfully
  Looking at the ring of bruises

That adorned my throat
And he said that
These magic drugs
Would help but
You would always be
More aggressive
While on them
And ever after
But they're there to help
Right?
It'll be fine.

The walls were pale green
And the windows were high
Windows that would not open
Because you weren't there
For a holiday
You were there
Because you were sick
Schizophrenia they said
And then they changed their mind
And said you have
A personality disorder
They can't fix you they said
You should get out, they said
Before he kills you
So help him, I said.
Before he does.

So many people in there
Rocking and crying and laughing
Screaming
I remember
The woman who wanted to save the world
And take us all to Egypt
So we would be safe
And she looked at me once
With love in her eye
And said that I need to stop
Being everything for everyone
And look after me for a change

There was a woman with
Anorexia on the ward
Getting help and support
Hugs on tap
Understanding when she ate
And I looked at her
And I knew that
Nobody noticed
When I couldn't eat in public
Or purged my food away
In secret
Getting rid of it
In anonymous toilets
So nobody would know

I felt envious of her.

You all wanted to get out
You hated the walls
You hated the group talks
The therapy
The calm voices
The locks and keys
And safe places to sleep

And sometimes
When I walked away
To go to work
And buy you more stuff
That you said you needed
And pay the bills
With only one wage
Instead of two
And worry about my studies
As the lecturers didn't know
And I wasn't going to tell them

Sometimes I admit
I wanted to get in
To be locked away
And looked after
And be safe within walls
Just for a while

So who was the mad one?
You, for wanting to get out
Or me, for wanting to get in?

A Refund

This is what you have cost me
   And I would like to itemise it
   For my refund
   Healthcare
   Continued healthcare in fact
   Including all the tests
   For my brain injury
   Thanks for that
   Roll neck jumpers
   It might seem trivial
   But I cannot now wear them
   As the material feels like
   Your hands not so tenderly
   Circling my throat
   As you squeezed so tight

   It's going on the list
   Also too my fractured vertebrae

That you shattered with your boot
In swinging kick as I curled up
To protect myself
And my bed, the bed that I saved for
That I paid for myself
That you burned to a cinder
As revenge because I got a place
In a refuge for a few nights
To get away from you
And your booze fuelled rages
That I had to pay for
As you didn't work anymore
I know you blamed me for that
But it's going on my claim

I don't suppose that my emotional
Wounds would count in a spreadsheet
For a claim of a refund
Because it's too wishy washy
So let's leave it at that

My Paypal is the usual email
Fuckyou@nomore.com
I'll spend the refund on
Useless stuff that you would
Have hated
Not that you still take up space
In my head

After all these years
That would be preposterous
Wouldn't it.

Those Days

Night falls and the stars awaken
  Carrying memory of ancient song
  Great heroes sit up there looking down
  And sometimes that brings me comfort.

  But they did not reach me in the dark days
  When my choices were more stark
  And I would drink to numb the pain
  Stumbling back to cold empty dark
  Or violence waiting with raised fist
  And knife gleaming fiercely sharp
  Blows raining down in an angry wind
  Sharp words wielded in rageful waves
  And when escaping that dark anger
  Still those stars could not save me
  Smiling faces holding a grim intent
  Moving pieces on the chessboard
  Waiting for me to be hemmed in

Waiting for me to surrender

Callused hands moving on my skin
Ignoring my head turned away
And cold-set face in fear
Hot breath hitched in my face

Muttered whispers float by
"Come on you owe me this"
"I'm not like those other guys"
"I won't hurt you you know"

But they still take and my heart
Ruptures into sparks of starlight
And I slip away softly
Leaving a statue with tear stains
Frozen in the past forever.

I seek the stars and this ancient song
And I fly away so high
High in the dark sky.

Sleep is Safe, Right?

I was supposed to be safe
  Sleeping at my friend's house
  On her sofa

  A woman who knew my trauma
  Who lived through
  Her own horrors
  And was making her way
  As best she could

  She wasn't to know
  That I woke up with

  A man's arm wrapped around my neck
  And the other down my pants
  Fingers delving
  Not letting me go

HIs breath tainting my ear
As he held me tighter once he knew
That I was awake, that I knew.

I fought and I bit
That hand that held me
And finally he freed me
His fingers falling away

As I fled the house
I ran out into the night
Not knowing where to go
Because nowhere was safe
Anymore.

I slept rough that night
In the driving rain
If you call it sleeping
When you keep one eye open

Because shutting them
Means that you cannot
Protect yourself.

She did not ask once
Why I was not there
When she woke in the morning

She never asked
Why I never stayed there
Again.

And I never spoke of it.
Not to her.
Not really to anyone.
Not until now.

Replay By The Book

I don't remember how it started
  What I did to cause it
  I remember how it ended
  You dragging me by my hair
  Screaming in my face

  My face pulsed with blame
  How could I
  How could I be in this again
  But pregnant

  I read all the books
  I did everything right
  I looked for red flags
  Yet here I was again
  The perfect man
  Who knew it all

Where I had been
And now I had created
A monster
His face contorted
Screaming,
"Is this what you want?"
I was wrong
Love isn't
For people like me

Sleeping

I was sleeping. I know that.
  I was safe
  We had been through this
  My tiresome trauma
  Getting in the way
  But then I woke
  Your eyes were soulless
  I said no
  I said no
  I fractured when it didn't matter
  No doesn't matter
  Frozen
  I loved you
  How could you

Mac

You died on a Thursday
  Prosaically
  A heart attack
  The Coroner said that
  You had something genetic maybe
  It was your time
  You would have laughed at that
  If you had been there
  At your own Inquest
  You were the only one
  The only decent one
  The best man
  Ripped away at 49
  Only my stepdad
  Not a big deal

Do You

Do you remember when we met?
  A meeting of minds, you said
  You wooed me with words
  Dancing the dance
  Perfectly
  Observing consent

  I was wooed
  I ignored the blazing
  Red flags
  I did ignore them
  I'm not worth it anyway
  I saw them
  But what did it matter anyway?

  It should have mattered
  We built a life
  Of sorts

If you call a fractured
Orbiting of planets
Fuelled by alcohol
A relationship

You did not hurt me
Of course you did the
Emotional stuff
The gaslighting
The usual
That's a relationship though
Normal

But then my dads died
My life unravelled
First Mac, my hero
The first man who I trusted
My stepfather
Dying quietly in a blaze of glory

And then a scant year later my da
Finally finding his way home
And you and I
I do not know if
You tired of me first
Wanting someone more
Biddable
Younger

Or if I saw again that this
Was doomed
But what I do know is
Despite your bragging in pubs
Kitty has had a hard life
She's never had a home of hers
I would never take it
And taking the praise,
Oh, you took the praise

You looked at me then
And you said, if you leave
I'll take the house
And frost descended
I moved out
You wanted to be the good guy
You said.

It didn't matter that
I found that house myself
That you moved in after
That you took it from me
It did not matter that again
I was homeless

You had to be the good guy, right?
How did that go?

How does it look, being the bad guy,
You asked me, once.
Epic, I said.

Becoming A Blank Page

Sometimes for me the world fragments
   And dissolves into fractures of glass
   I don't always see it coming
   I can be living obliviously and then
   My brain buckles under the strain.

   It does not matter how you battle
   By words or sword or by smile
   You have to give up, you will
   As your brain disintegrates
   No charm or prayer will help this
   You can not escape it.
   The inevitability.

   Thoughts crawl through my mind
   Like they struggle through mud
   Reaching out desperately but slow
   The delay of thoughts, the echo

As they shout in desperation so loud
But the brain withers and slows
It doesn't understand the warning
As language loses its meaning.

My eyes lose focus then, and still
I look at nothing. I am frozen.
My facial muscles become as lead
Slack, expressions falling like hail
Limbs shake and resist but submit
All must be still now.

But my thoughts jump from jagged edge
Left to right, in nervous rage
Trapped within a statue of skin
Then even that collapses on itself
My brain slows and stutters to a stop
A breath, only. Breathe. Breathe.

Time breathes too, in its own time
Not measured by seconds or minutes
But by breath, a slow exhale of the clock
And that is how I am ruled in the blank
Of the page, where my face sits empty
My hands strewn carelessly where they fell
And I wait for life to return to me from the void.

There is nothing but the wait, the husk

Of body and bone and sinew that sits
Without a spark of something to move it
But slowly like a spring thawing
The life returns to my face, reaching down
From my cheekbones to my mouth
And I inhale strong, like I am starved
And blood rushes to my bones again.

You Drive Fast When You're Angry

You drive fast, that you know
   You should know as I have told you
   My hands gripping the seat
   Knuckles going white
   And you speed up, more and more.

   My face freezes with fear
   As you weave past cars
   Your face intent on the road
   Snarl ever present, ready to bite

   This is our punishment
   For making you angry
   You pay back with fear
   An ounce of annoyance
   Means a pound of terror
   I'm sure it seems fair.
   To you

You drive fast, faster still
Beeping at cars and swearing
Your hands slapping and hitting
Tearing at the wheel
Pulling at the road
Fighting car drivers
Scaring us

But I cannot speak up again
The last time was disastrous
With my face being shoved
Into the car window
And you screaming in my ear
And I thought we were
Going to die

Maybe you wanted that
I don't know
So I do not speak
But I hold the seat
I pay the tax
The punishment
For annoying you
I do not speak
As you drive so fast
Because you are angry
And so you drive fast.

Walking on Eggshells

You say to me
  That you have to walk
  On eggshells
  Because I ask you to stop
  Calling me names
  And to stop throwing things
  To stop shouting at me
  Just because I disagree

You say to me
  That it isn't fair
  That you should not have to
  Think about what you say
  Because you would not be angry
  If I just did things better
  And did as I was told
  And stop making you angry

I say to you
That we get frightened
When you shout so suddenly
And throw things about
When you shove and push
When you glare hatefully

I say to you
That we walk on eggshells
We sense your mood change
In an instant
When something angers you
And we all become more careful
To get things right

I say to you
That once you were kind
And safe to be around
And we weren't frightened
Before you changed

But you say to me
That you will not be changed
And you are the one
Who has to walk on eggshells
Because I make you angry
And you are not allowed
To rage freely

That I should change
And be better
And do better
And then you would not
Have to be angry
And walk over eggshells again.

Gaslighting

It's a sharpened tool
  That you only bring out
  When I start to assert myself again
  When my clarity returns for a while
  When I grasp the reins of myself
  And then you begin

  The unravelling
  Words are uttered at me
  Spitting hate in phrases
  And when I ask you calmly
  To not insult me again
  You deny it.
  You need your hearing checked
  You sneer.
  Can't you understand English?

  You wage silent war

Over shopping lists
Leaving out one crucial item
That then you desperately need
And you wave the list at me
Right in my face
Saying, can't you read?
I silently produce the evidence
A photograph of the original list
Before you wrote the item in later
And you call me paranoid
Because why would you do that?

You touch me
On my leg, my waist
Even though I asked you not to
And you tell me that
I am worthless now
As I cannot trust
And understand the difference
Between what you do
And what men did to me long ago
That they might be wrong
But you are in the right

You use my words against me
And tell me that I twist your words
That I am gaslighting you
That I am an abuser

And finally I unravel, wondering
And I am silenced
My tongue shuts down
And I don't know any more.

Am I the one?
Am I gaslighting?
And then you smile
It is a worthy tool indeed
A sharp one that slices
My sanity cleanly in two
And I unravel
In my doubt. Is it me?
Am I really gaslighting?

The Silencing Rule

My tongue holds itself still
  With such violence
  Clamped to the roof of my mouth
  I wonder if it will bruise itself
  The marks of shackles of fear

  Don't say anything
  Stay quiet when the slamming starts
  The vehemence spat from lips
  The breaking of things, my things

  Responses must not break through
  The shield of my mouth, shuttered
  The violence without and within
  Will overpower me, flood-like

  I pry my tongue from the roof
  Of my imprisonment

Numbing it and laying it gently
In its bed to sleep
Shutting doors softly
Cocooning myself from within.

Voiceless

When your throat burns
   And the edges of your eyes
   Feel as if they will explode
   From the rage that needs
   To leap out of you
   But you say nothing
   Because there is nothing else to say

   When someone you thought
   Was a friend, an ally
   Systematically humiliates you
   And your heart aches from it
   But you say nothing
   Because there is nothing else to say

   When someone hurts you
   With a well-placed jab
   They did not know that it

Landed true and deep
But you say nothing
Because there is nothing else to say

When someone pushes
Hard on your boundaries
At your NO point
They know that you hate it
And they do it anyway
But you say nothing
Because there is nothing else to say

When you feel the rage bubbling
And the tears forming
And you don't know what to do
And you want to scream
From the despair
But you say nothing
Because there is nothing else to say.

That is voiceless.
I am voiceless
I gave up my voice
So long ago
And now I have nothing else to say.

I Do Not
Understand

I do not understand
  How you can smile
  As if there is still
  Something there
  When you spit insults
  At me like you have
  Directed a cannon at me

I do not understand
Why you will not let me leave
When you do not actually want
Your children near you
Unless you are in public
But I cannot take them home
For a life without you
Without fear

I do not understand

Your rapid mood swings
That begin to scare me now
I feel the collective freeze
When you shout
And I mourn the person
You once used to be

I do not understand.
Perhaps you are right
That I am just that stupid
I am holding half a page
Making sense of one side
And I am asking.
Help me understand?

You Give Me A Rose

You give me a rose
　A gleamingly soft bloom
　With puckering petals
　And a soft fragrance
　And I am supposed to gasp
　And lean in and sniff
　And say thank you, right?
　But I cannot do that
　I see a rose
　And I look for a blade.

　I know this sounds ungrateful
　And to you it probably is
　But when I see a kind gesture
　I look for the sting
　I look for the hurt that is waiting
　I look for the cost.

This is the blade a-waiting
This is what I am used to
A gift always has a cost
A smile always has a knife
A compliment always has its price.

So when you smile and kiss
When you lean in to say
I love you
I might smile
But I am looking for the blade -
I am waiting.

I know that this
Is from my tortured past
That I should let it lie
Slumbering in dreams
But that isn't how it works
I am a Pavlovian nightmare
Not of my own making
But there it is.

Know that I will love the rose
I will love that you give it
But my eyes will dance
Around to seek out
That dark blade
Because for me

In my nightmares still
It is there, waiting.
So have patience with me.
Please.

'You Learn That Being Lonely Is The Price For Being Safe'

Lonely isn't so bad you know
  It can even be quite nice
  You're a one body
  In between a sea of twos
  Rushing past you in a stream
  Flowing by you as if
  You are a repelling magnet
  There to quell their hopes
  Of perpetual coupledom

  For me lonely is the price
  I willingly pay the toll
  Because the phrase is true

It is the price for being safe

I become subsumed in a couple
My brain drowns under the stimulus
The shoulds and shouldn'ts
The sighs and the caresses

I lose a sense of myself
And for some that is just perfect
Because then you can be shaped
And moulded and trained and cowed
To choose lonely, and alone
Or choose fists flailing down
Silence forced down your throat
The doors slamming shut
As you realise that
You have nowhere to go
I choose lonely.

That is my price and I pay it
I smile as I drop the coins into
The gloved hand of the collector
Because that is the price
For being safe
Because people like me
Have no choice but to take it
But I will take it
And I will be glad of it.

Triggers

A trigger always reminds me
  Of a gun, gleaming
  Its shot coming loud and fast
  And the world has changed

  My triggers seem to be small
  The last grain of sand or rice
  That lands on top of me and
  I feel as if I cannot breathe
  It is impossible to tell
  When it's coming
  The exact moment

  I would like to know
  So I can prepare
  For when I shift from normal
  To something other
  But I cannot.

They come thick and fast
And then not for ages
So much like buses
I can function so well
For so long
And then I am aching
In my soul
Anger warring with tears
Hot wet flashes
Rolling down my cheeks
Even while I grit my teeth
Hating the world

Promises broken
Being let down yet again
Having to shift from
What I know is right
Not being able to protect
My loved ones
I have to let go and care less
To not expect from people
To not hope for better
Because these are my triggers
And I want to take the
Bullets from the gun
I want to stop feeling again.

I Just Don't Fit

I don't, really
  And I have made my peace with it
  I try so hard
  But I can't quite catch the rhythm
  I'm one beat off somehow
  And people look over
  Strangely
  And I know that I made
  Another misstep
  It's not like I try to be edgy
  Or different

  Actually I have always dreamed
  Of being normal
  But I made my peace with it
  I can't manage that somehow
  At times people think of me as
  Eccentric and edgy but still you know

In the realms of normal
And those are the days when I think
I made it happen today.

But more often I hit the jangling tone
I walk the wrong line
And I walk away knowing
That I didn't find my tribe today
And as long as I didn't upset anyone
Everything is good
But still
Once in a while it would be nice
To feel like I was part of a tribe too.

Is It Me?

Some days the burdens
  Are heavy to carry
  It feels like the past
  Is gnawing at my heart
  The ghosts are pulling at me
  And I feel as if I have not
  Made any progress at all
  Some days people's voices
  Are more caustic than usual
  And I do all the right things
  Asking if they meant it
  Saying that I think I might
  Be feeling sensitive but...

  Is it me?
  Perhaps I am just too sensitive
  Some days
  Perhaps my wounds gape open

Sometimes
And the hurt comes sliding in
Wrenching tears from my eyes
Painfully
But my questions are dismissed
If I ask, is it me?

I get told, yes it is
And so I have to accept
That the hurtful things
People say are funny or ironic
That the insults aren't real
That I misheard them
Or I am being sensitive
Hormonal

Is it me?
Because I wouldn't want
To think that I was hurting people
So I tie myself in knots
To make sure my people
Are kept safe from me
From my cruel words
And at times I can be
Cruel

But sometimes
It feels as if

Adulting means
Adults can tantrum
And blaze and hurt
And insult
And pass it off as jest
But only if it isn't me
Because I can't do that.
And so I am wondering
Is it me?

Kind Things People Say

I'm at the bus station
  Hoping to get home
  As I finished work an hour ago
  And it's late, I'm tired
  It's Friday and the pubs are busy
  And the catcalls are flowing strong.

  I'm in a long dress and a jacket
  For the record,
  Not that it should matter.
  Hey do you want to fuck?
  Stop ignoring us! Nice tits!
  And it continues. I'm 17.

  I'm sitting waiting for my pizza
  Hot and sweaty from the night club
  With big wide army pants
  A hat and a huge jacket

For the record,
Not that it should matter.

Some guy repeatedly shouts
To get my attention
And then asks
How much for a blowjob?
And gets annoyed with me
When I don't get on my knees
But instead I square up for a fight
Because honestly,
I should be flattered. I'm 27.

I'm reading a book at the train station
Minding my own business
Wearing jeans and a jacket
For the record
Not that it should matter

And some guy comes up to ask
What am I reading
Then asks if I am married
And tells me that he wants
To take me home and ravish me
And gets angry
When I am not grateful
For his kind offer. I'm 31.

I was cycling home
Wearing trousers and a jacket
For the record
Not that it should matter

When two men in a car
Drive next to me
Shouting
Hey bitch
Hey you fucking slut
How about riding us
You dirty fucking whore

And they tell me to
Fuck off and die
When I give them the finger
And tell them to go fuck themselves
Because honestly
A woman should be more polite. I'm 37.

I was walking
In the street with my friend
Wearing a summer dress
And a man walks past
And calls me a dirty slut

And my friend tells me
That I should be flattered

And not threaten to punch him
Because I shouldn't wear a dress
If I don't want to invite
That kind of behaviour.
Who knew. I'm 22.

Manspreader

The bus is busy
   Packed with tired commuters
   And screaming children
   And dead-eyed teens
   You come to sit next to me
   One of the few seats left
   To claim the remaining half

   You sit, you wriggle, you stretch
   Then your leg starts to press
   Trying to edge me into the window
   Your thigh getting closer to me
   Touching mine
   My skin crawls with the contact
   An enforced intimacy with a stranger
   And you look straight ahead
   Not acknowledging my look
   Nor my raised eyebrow.

You push some more,
Leaning against my leg
With all your strength
And I put all my weight
Into my leg making it stone
Filling the muscles and sinews
With cement. I will not surrender
My seat and cower against
A window so you can have more room
I'm stubborn like that, you see.

We battle like that for a while
Your face getting angrier
Your leg pushing harder
And I sit, resolute
We can do this all day.
Your stop arrives and you exhale
A furious gust of breath
And you stand to leave
But before you go
You look at me and your lip curls
Fucking bitch, you say.
I smile. You're welcome
I reply.

Man On The Bus

The bus was empty
  Seats yawning from front to back
  I was at the back of course
  And you headed right for me
  Sitting right next to me
  On my seat
  And I leaned away
  As far as I could from you
  Wanting to be alone
  And you knew that

  You chided me gently
  For being impolite
  For showing my discomfort
  At a stranger sharing my space
  The heat of your leg burning mine.

  The questions started

Do you have a boyfriend?
I'm 15, I said.
That doesn't matter, he said
Do you want a boyfriend?
No I don't, I said
And he laughed
Breathing his air over me
Good plan sweetheart, he said
You need a real man

I smiled weakly back
Not knowing what to say
As nobody had prepared me
And there was nobody there
To intervene.

You did not touch me
You talked and you pried
And you enjoyed my discomfort
Getting as close as you could
And eventually after so long
You left, heaving yourself to your feet
Lurching down the bus

And my seat felt empty
I did not know how to reclaim
My space
I almost missed it

The discomfort that you caused
Because feeling something
Even if it's bad
Is better than feeling nothing at all

Deluxe

My face does not reflect
   In the mirror
   Indolent viewing
   Is reserved for the
   Deluxe faces

   Those who were born
   With a spoon of gold
   Soft feather pillows
   Joy fed intravenously

   I was thrown
   Into a squalling winter
   A wind of discontent
   Battered and bruised
   Edges chipped

   I was never the

Luxury model
Gleaming corners
Chrome faces
Perfect paint

I was the screaming
Wheel held together
By angst and string
I do not look in the mirror
I do not look at my lack

But I do not now
Revile it
My standardness
My economy of motion
I do not look
But I live, just as I am.

My Own Nightmare

Your smile rasps against yet young scars
   Wincing at open invisible wounds
   Not that it matters
   Because you didn't mean it
   You triggered me today.

   You certainly didn't mean to
   Making suggestions as to why
   Technology failed so dramatically
   And I fulfilled your suggestions

   Feeling the fear rise
   As it did not work
   I did not create it
   But I lived the fear for it
   I could see it
   But I could also see
   Fist fights raining in blood

When the remote control stopped
Because I had made it so
Once

I was the villain but also the victim
Punches raining down fast
For my transgression
And today somehow you stepped
Into that zone
You did nothing wrong
You did not speak out of turn
You were not angry
Not terrifying

But still something took me there
To a place of horror
A place maybe that I never left
It was not your fault
Not your fault when I exited
Not your fault
Not my fault either
But it will take me centuries
To believe that lie

My Fixes

A Memory

It was never well lit
  Which is why I had been
  Grabbed there once before
  I stood around for a while
  Knowing I had to walk through
  Not knowing what to do
  And I acted stupidly

  I saw a guy, a big guy
  And I went to him
  And I said,
  I have to get to my bus stop
  And I'm scared, I got attacked here
  Can you help me?
  He looked down at me
  This big bear of a man
  And he said, how old are you?
  I'm 16, I said.

I still remember what he said
You're the same age as my sister.
Come on. He gave me his arm
He enveloped me into his world
He walked me to my bus stop
He didn't ask me why I wasn't safe
He didn't try his luck with a scared kid

He just took me to the bus stop
And watched me get on with worried eyes
Before he walked away
I never had the chance to tell him
That to me he was an angel

And nearly thirty years on
He still is
I don't even know his name
But he was an angel who
Stepped in for me once
And I will never forget him
I will never stop
Being grateful

I Wore A Wedding Ring

I wore a ring on my finger
   From when I was 17
   I bought a cheap silver ring
   From the bazaar where I worked
   Plain, round, not fancy
   And I slipped it onto my left hand
   I married myself.

   It was my cape of invisibility
   I could move my hand subtly
   And eyes would fall onto it
   And they would move away
   Oh you're married?
   I would nod, nonchalantly
   And the hunting light in their eye
   Would dim and they would cast about
   For their next catch
   Leaving me with an overflowing ashtray

And the ends of a cheap pint
For the barmaid to clear away.

I wore it even when I was in love
Entwined and enmeshed
My hopes fluttering over eyelashes
And strong arms and smiles
I kept it on because they didn't mind
If men left me alone

I changed that silver band eventually
For something a bit more
In keeping with my finances
Switching to white gold for a while
A ring from the jeweller this time
And the clerk raised his eyebrow
At the silence next to me
The empty space where a husband
Should be
When I am buying a wedding ring
But my money was good
And he didn't care that much.

I wore a ring through marriage
And through divorce
The people I did not know
Did not know that the ring
Was a sham, a pretence

Those who did know me
Knew why it mattered
And they did not mind

I changed the ring again
For a plain rose gold one
Bevelled and plain and thin
Switching it to my right hand
When I packed up and moved countries
Because in my new country
The wives wore a ring on their right
There might be a language barrier
But the behaviour is the same
The lighting of interest
The spark of the hunt
Which dies away when
They see the gold gleaming
On your hand
I'm possessed by another
It says quietly
And they pass you by

It's my cape of invisibility
That has served me
For over two decades
Which is now my only
Metal adornment
I have my own weapons now

My boundaries are strong and high
I can quell a hunter with a look
But I still keep my cape
Of invisibility
I keep it close
And I keep it safe.

Patriarchy
Chicken

I heard about the phrase somewhere
  And thought it sounded delightful
  It boils down to not moving out of the way
  Of approaching men
  When walking in the street
  As we're taught to do
  And seeing what happens

I'm a fan of chicken personally
  Patriarchy and otherwise
  So I decided to adopt it
  And I stepped out into the wild
  Shoulders squared and ready.

It is a hard thing to do
  To stop your feet deftly darting
  Out of the way
  Into oncoming traffic

Or into a puddle maybe

It's become a habit
But I stop doing it
I walk on, taking the pavement
Just my part, nothing extravagant
Just my space walking by

I was not prepared for the rage
That the empty space was not available
That instead of them flowing freely
Not thinking just walking

They encountered me
Just walking, just being there
Curses flew past my ear
Insults spat with venom

Sometimes a shoulder would jut out
To knock me off centre
Anger spilling around me
All that heated rage
Could have cooked me a chicken
In my daily walk to work
Patriarchy or otherwise
Fancy that.

Black Roses

A song unleashing echo
   And untapped rage responds
   Melody that bridges old grief
   The pure voice sings of sorrow
   A fracturing in the soul
   Precious memory rises slowly
   And holds hands with wisdom
   There are ashes of regret to gather
   And gently lay them to rest
   To call the keening ghosts home
   As a plaintive voice caresses
   Through electronic soundwaves
   I am not under your spell
   She sings.
   I shake off the melody
   I let go of the memory
   I walk away free, and lighter.

Pain Takes Away Pain

Shattered glass gleaming
   Uttering a quiet promise
   In its sharp gleaming edges
   Pain takes pain away.

   Pain is still pain, this is true
   A burning pain from dark shards
   Can wash away a frozen hurt.
   Pain can bring forth anger
   And wash away the blur
   Of hot prismed tears that fall
   And sit in the edge of my eyes
   It clarifies me, it burns away
   All the doubts. The fears.

   A furious determination sits
   And replaces the numb fear.
   The blade once dragged hard

Against soft, yielding flesh
And that angry burn, the heat
It made my breath hiss out
In an exhale of relief. It is gone.

That white hot pain burned
In searing lines on my skin
It eased the cold feelings
And the mantra whispered on
"Don't believe in anyone"
"Don't believe in anything"

When the dark beckons me now
Sometimes my fingers twitch
In an empty familiar gesture
It's almost a reckless flex
My hands remembering the past
And how it felt to drag in anger
The pain out of my weeping body
And watching the blood red tears
Spring up out of my torn skin.

Do I miss it, now, so long after
When I sit alone in the dark?
Sometimes yes, I still miss it.
Because pain takes pain away
And now my heart keens faintly
Shrouded as it is in dark shadow.

I Wish For A Time Machine

The concept whirrs and sits
In my over-fevered brain and
Yet I think over it, the impact
Of a time machine. Of my.
Time machine. Mine.
Where would I go?
What would I change?
What would I take away?
And what would I give back?
Would I stay within my own life
Tinkering at the frayed edges
With the wisdom of hindsight
Offering advice in timely eyes
Pushing my younger self
To go on slightly different roads?
Would I take away the sorrow
The pain, the hot blooded tears?
Would I take away the mistakes

That make me who I am now?
Would I go forward, just to look
And see if I make it there,
If I am happy, really happy?
If I am, would I steal the formula
And whisper it to my past self
And change my life throughout?
I wonder what I would ask myself.
If I would ask what I did right
And what I did so very wrong
But most of all I wonder.
Would I forgive myself, finally?
Is a time machine so powerful
That it can make me forgive me?
Can I accept my scars, my tears
And allow myself to move on?
I wonder. I wonder.

Nourish

A faltering feeling
  Emerges
  Dread rises
  Nourish requires me
  To replace the
  Clearheadedness
  With satiety
  Fast to slow
  But my limbs will it
  My mind stutters
  From the wish
  To nourish is to
  Stop and listen
  And remedy
  To wash away
  Our angst
  To feed deep
  When we hunger

To fill long
When we thirst
To touch
When we shiver
So alone.

Depression

I remember once
  Someone hearing my
  Obsession with sad music
  And they cocked their head
  So delicately
  As they told me that it was
  All very depressing.

  I do not know if I had realised
  Before then, that some do not
  Consider depression to be their
  Companion, if you will.
  Some walk with it all their life
  Some do not.
  Should we run from it?
  If we did, perhaps bands
  And songwriters and poets
  Would have a harder time

If all their poetry was
Pontificating about clouds
And slushies and such like
Cheerful things

Would the world be a better place?
Or do we need to keep our
Wonderful writers in that space
So they write us sublime agony
That we can screen and quote
Smile over, and walk away

I approach it today
As an old friend
The melancholy
Approaches gently
Bringing me memory
Understanding
The feeling mellows me
Takes the edge off
From the shriek of the grind

Today it does not prostate me
Today it does not dissect me
Today it is mellow
Something soft and sophisticate
A gentle sorrow
Something I am grateful for

Almost
For someone from the outside
They would see smiles and content
Who sees the real me?
Depression does.
Perhaps I should give it more credit.

Putting Me Together

A sob breaks from my lips
   Like a wave bursting
   And she asked
   Her face furrowed
   Her eyes filled with concern
   What's wrong, mama?

   I lied and said it was
   Just pain in my hip
   But she was not fooled
   That evening when I
   Kissed her good night
   So fresh from her bath
   She put her little arms
   Around me and
   SQUEEZED

   As if she could put me

Back together again
And I think she did
Just a little bit.

You

Again my eye is drawn
   To the curve of your mouth
   I look back up
   Reluctantly
   Dragging my eye
   To meet yours
   Seeing that light within
   Your steady regard
   And I smile
   Feeling the edges of my lip
   Tug
   In response to yours
   Your smile
   That smile that lifts me
   The one that I cannot avoid
   Just like you
   The one that I cannot turn from
   The one that I irrevocably need

My fingers flex, just once
Dreaming of tracing the line
The curve of your mouth
Your jaw
Seeing the spark of light
Spring from your eyes
I smile
And my hand falls away.

Poet Warriors

Warriors who hang up their swords
  Taking up instead with gnarled fingers
  Dark ink poured into dessicated hearts
  Fingers flex and flow, hearing the rhythm
  Yet not knowing how to frame it
  But then they straighten as the Sun rises
  The melody falls like a stone
  Around, splintering the dawn
  And they understand at last
  They write. They write with hands
  They write with their hearts
  They bleed ink onto pages
  And when they are done
  Spilling their soul into verse
  They turn, bowing once to the Sun
  And melt away into the breeze.

Is it Love

I can't believe it is,
   You know that
   We went into this friends first
   Both desperately not wanting to
   Ruin what we had
   Afraid

   That I know is true
   I know you would walk over fire
   For me
   Perhaps if you knew who I actually was
   You would not,
   Or perhaps I do not
   Give you enough credit

   I don't speak enough
   I am locked away behind layers
   Of masks

Defensiveness
Fear lies behind the anger
I know this hurts you

You will not push
If I put up the barriers you won't
Step closer
I do not ask you to
I am not a good person to love
But you do anyway

I do too
Love you that is
Even in my days of loathing
When I don't know the difference
Between night and day
When horror fractures my dreams
I still know you
That I love you

Is it real?
I hope it is
As much as I can hope
As much as someone like me
Can hope
I am but an empty bottle
Drained dry
A weapon

But within those sharp grains
There is a star
The tiniest spark
Against the odds
My heart knows you
And I think that might mean
This is
Love
Maybe

Embrace the Chaos

Embrace it
  As if it were that easy
  To detach myself
  From the delicate maelstrom
  To remove myself
  And turn to take it in my arms
  The chaos is embedded deep
  It rages within me
  I march in straight lines
  Planting plans in edges
  Determined to stamp order
  Into my chaotic inner world
  But the desert laughs hollow
  As it will not be changed
  Absorbed into sanity
  I cannot embrace the chaos
  I am merely part of it
  Chaos is part of me.

Walking Alone

Life is not about
   Walking in someone's shadow
   Fulfilling their dreams
   First
   Because they always come
   First

   It's about seeing clearly
   Where you have to go
   And seeing if they will
   Stop
   And look at how they can
   Adjust their course to
   Incorporate yours.

   Life is not about
   Serving one person
   Giving yourself up

It's about being you
Just you
Walking alone
Together

Therapy

Therapy isn't a comfortable chair
   With a prim face in front of me
   Trying to understand who I am
   Trying to make me understand
   Who I am
   There is worth in this
   I do not deny
   But I hide behind layers of masks
   Sabotaging myself

   Therapy is putting my face into the wind
   Cycling so fast I feel I can fly
   Letting the inner child take the front seat
   For a little while, nurturing them in a way
   They never got in real life
   Therapy is running, the solid beat of feet
   On streets, the music in my ears

Therapy is naming my feelings as I feel them
Painstakingly identifying. I feel ... today.
Stumbling over something that my
Sweet 5 year old can do with ease
But my tongue is beginning to say
I feel... today.
That is better than not feeling at all.

Therapy is knowing when to sleep
Because the world feels as if it is ending
Or to shower
Because I want to peel off my skin
In a fit of savage loathing
Therapy is knowing when I am going too far
Stepping into compulsions
And pushing it all back

Therapy is about learning to love
Peeling back the layers of masks little by little
Letting in the light just a little
Airing the scars just a little
Letting people listen, just a little

Therapy is writing my trauma down
Giving it to the air, to the sky
Bleeding out ink on pages
Howling my screams into paper
And then putting it away

Carefully
I do not always need to carry it
Dissect it

Therapy is about forgiving myself
For being a child
For not being superhuman
For learning how to not feel pain
For learning how to not feel at all
For co-dependency and dependence
On anything that would numb me
For trauma bonding
For over-sharing and under-sharing
For not trusting anyone
For not trusting myself

Therapy is about taking one day at a time
And doing the best I can with it
Because at the end of the day
I am still here, with me, myself
And that's actually just fine.

Two Sisters

One strong
　On the outside
　Sinews and muscle
　The roar of a lion

　One strong
　On the inside
　Loyalty carved deep
　The smile of a shark

　Two hearts
　One looking up
　In awe
　One looking down
　In love

　Two humans
　Flying high

Hair in the wind
Eyes meeting
Hearts smiling
Two sisters.

Scars – An Acrostic

Slices of rage roar loud
   Clustered around my pain
   Armour
   Rip me open, I'll add more
   Strength roams in scars

This Is My Life

This is my life
   It is not what I expected
   I had not planned this out
   Not the hurt or tears or joy
   And I had not seen the turns
   That sent me here and there
   But I approve of it. It is mine.

These are my dreams
   Hidden so close from everyone
   Afraid to blossom and grow
   Even in a cold winter storm
   But my dreams fought on
   And battled my own fears
   And I approve of it. They are mine.

These are my words
   Blunt and raw and exposed

Trailing from dream into scream
Sometimes in a perfect instant
But my pen became my hero
And I approve of it. They are mine.

And this is the smile
That shines out so unexpectedly
When the people closest to me
Reach out and light it up.
Those who know me best
Who rankle and love and protect
Pushing me into new realities
Forcing me into new impossible dreams
Showing me a myriad of lives.
And I approve of it. It is mine.

Acknowledgments

I would like to thank those who encouraged me to post this collection, who kept reminding me that raw and dark poetry needs to be seen too. There are so many warriors out there who are open about their struggles with mental health - I am not one of them. I am in awe of people who can be open about mental health, and act as a beacon to encourage others. We need to talk more about mental health, and about how it affects us. Being depressed, or living with PTSD, or whatever else, is not something to be ashamed about. So I thank them for standing up for the rest of us.

I also want to thank those who have helped bring this book from the shambles it started out as to where it is now. That includes the beta readers, the sharp-eyed foxes who spot my errors and errant commas, and it also includes my editor and my cover designer. I thank them each time because they're amazing. I'll keep thanking them.

And last, I appreciate my family, both my blood and my heart family, those who have brought me into their world. You are the reason why I am who I am now. You are my fixes. You are what makes life worthwhile.

About The Poet

Eryn was born and raised in Oxford, UK but nowadays lives in South Germany with their young family. They have a great dream to travel and visit all the great mountains and lakes of the world. They are a qualified History and English teacher, working freelance with international students.

They have been writing poetry since they were 16, including Middle-Earth fan poetry that has appeared with alarming regularity in the Tolkien Society's publication, the Amon Hen. They have also appeared in the Music Anthology from the Sweety Cat Press.

PTSD is a Four Letter Word is the third publication by Eryn, their former poetry collections are Of Swans And Stars, and Love Lost And Found. They are currently working on two new poetry collections, one which is about knowing ourselves and our masks, called Masquerade Me, and one about Gothic Horror, as yet untitled. They will both be released in 2023.

In addition to writing poetry they study with the Order of Bards, Ovates and Druids to be a druid, and are working on a few novels. The Sunset Sovereign, which is a dystopian fantasy about dragons, will be released early 2023, and they are currently writing a Gothic Horror novel about a sentient, feral bookshop, called The Black Cat Bookshop. There is also a steampunk fantasy novella idea about an Adventurer called Brontes which is being annoyingly persistent.

Printed in Great Britain
by Amazon

19883475R00099